SOAR ABOVE ADVERSITIES

Inspirational Poems that Uplift the Spirit

NADENE COOPER KING

SOAR ABOVE ADVERSITIES

Inspirational Poems that Uplift the Spirit

NADENE COOPER KING

PUBLISHED BY:
BRENTWOOD CHRISTIAN PRESS
4000 BEALLWOOD AVENUE
COLUMBUS, GEORGIA 31904

DEDICATION

This book is dedicated to:
My Heavenly Father, the one who birthed these poems in my
heart

• • •

My parents, the late Leaston and Elnora Cooper.

• • •

My in laws, the late John and Susie King

• • •

My husband John, and four sons Dr. John David, Dr. Samuel
Taylor, Kenneth Lorenzo and Jarvis Clay King and my three
daughters in law: Pearl, Bernadette and Stephanie King.

• • •

My family, friends and readers

• • •

All of God's children.

A NOTE TO READERS

This book is written for you in hopes that it will encourage, inspire, and motivate you to dig deep within and discover your God given abilities, and soar to greater heights knowing that He has equipped you with what it takes to overcome any adversity the world hurls your way. With the wind at your back and God propelling you, there is nothing that can hold you back. Because you are being backed up by the one who made you in His own image and in His likeness. You are worth your weight in gold! So allow me to admonish you, encourage you, and compel you to soar, soar; the sky is the limit! The world doesn't know it yet, but you have already arrived!

THE REAL DEAL
DARE TO BELIEVE!*

With God in your life, YOU CAN SOAR AS AN EAGLE!

You are fearfully and wonderfully made.

Greater is He that is in you than he that is in the world.

God will supply all of your need according to His riches in glory by Christ Jesus.

No weapon formed against you shall prosper.

Nothing is impossible with God.

You are more than a conqueror through Him who loves you.

If you trust God with all your heart and not depend on your understanding, He will determine your destiny.

Jesus died for your healing, spirit, mind, body and soul.

When you were born, you were born to fulfill a special purpose.

*The statements above are based on my understanding of God's Holy Word.

CONTENTS

SOAR ABOVE ADVERSITIES

AN INVENTORY

Have you discovered
That you are too weak to soar,
Don't have any energy,
No willpower any more?

Your mind is confused.
You feel frustrated,
Can't stand much pressure
Unless you get aggravated?

Your palms are sweaty.
You don't feel right.
Hate fuming inside.
You want to fight.

You have very little money,
No job at all,
Can't chance climbing because
You are afraid you'll fall.

All your life
You've been pushed around.
You have no reason to smile,
Too hurt to frown.

If all these things
Represent how you feel
Then read on my friend.
Your change is here.

As you read this book
As you read each line,
Get a grip on yourself.
Renew your mind.

Take in the thoughts
Word by word.
Try to meditate
On everything you've heard.

Then when you have read
This whole book through.
There'll be no more confusion.
You'll know the real you!

CONSCIENCE SPEAKS

Yesterday was a struggle.
Yesterday I labored.
Today I feast
And eat from a table

Which is laden with humility
And loads of dignity.
Because I've put forth my best effort.
I did it all for *me.*

When the task grew hard
I persisted.
When the wind blew against me
I resisted.

Sometimes along the way
I wanted to hesitate.
But conscience said, "Do it now.
Don't procrastinate.

If you have a job to do
Do it with determination.
Be a go-getter.
Build a solid foundation."

Conscience kept on speaking
In the back of my head.
I could not ignore
The things conscience said.

So I opened my ears
To what it had to say.
"First get busy.
Get started on your way.

While others are being sidetracked
You focus on the task at hand,
Set your own goals.
You must have a plan.

Never neglect your duties.
Work until they're done.
Make your decision today.
You have a race to run.

Run like there's no tomorrow.
Run like it is your last day.
Be strong; be determined.
Let nothing stand in your way.

No one can take your place.
No one can run for you.
You must chart your own course.
You must run at your own pace.

And when your journey is over
And you must take your test.
Don't ever be ashamed of the outcome
As long as you've done your best."

EMPTY YOUR SACK

Take hold of the plow of life.
You'll lose ground if you look back.
Get rid of the stuff that's holding you down.
Start unloading your sack

Of wishing and wanting
And all that self doubt.
Reach down into your sack.
Throw "I can't " out.

Get rid of lack
And life is too hard.
Throw out last year's problems.
Begin a new start.

Empty your sack of slothfulness
And blaming someone else.
Throw out hindrance of any kind;
Even forgive yourself

Of the times that you could have
And the times you failed but tried.
Dispose of everything that is garbage.
Stop giving waste a free ride.

Lift up your head.
Let the real you come through.
Straighten up your shoulders.
Do what is expected of you.

Now that you have rid yourself
Of the stuff that was in your sack,
Run like the dickens.
Let nothing hold you back.

You are a conqueror.
Start working toward your destiny.
Keep struggling; keep striving
Until you gain your victory.

YOU ARE A WINNER

Don't think negatively.
Think positively instead.
You are not the tail.
You are the head.

You were born with
All the qualities you need
Not to fail,
But to succeed.

All you need to do
Is to do your very best.
Never give up
If you want success.

If you quit
You lose by default.
You did not stay the course
And keep trying as you ought.

If you have to work
Until the early morn,
Never give up
Until the task is done.

Don't let obstacles
Ruin your dreams.
Things are not always
As they seem.

You have what it takes.
It is in your soul.
Don't settle for peanuts.
Go for the gold.

When the race is over
And you've done your best.
Go home and relax.
Feel free to rest.

Hard work pays off.
It brings you front and center.
When you do your best
You are always a WINNER!!!

LET GO OF EGYPT

Let go of your Egypt.
Leave it behind.
Let go of your Egypt.
Renew your sick mind.

A new day is dawning
Right before your eyes.
Stop thinking about Egypt.
Take hold of the prize.

Your past imprisonment
Remember it no more.
Turn it lose.
There are better things in store.

Your Egypt left your body
With bruises and with scars.
Get a view of better days ahead.
Fix your eyes upon the stars.

Old things are passing away.
New things are in sight.
Step on the road of restoration.
Turn from darkness into light.

The Father is waiting
With his outstretched hand.
He wants you to leave Egypt
And inhabit a better land.

A land flowing with health and prosperity,
And opportunities galore.
Let go of your Egypt.
Never return anymore.

There is so much in life
That is at your beacon call.
Leave the land of bondage.
Begin to scale the wall.

The wall of success awaits you
If you only have the faith to try.
Let go of all your Egypts.
Let your old habits die.

You have it in your grasp
The ability to succeed.
Let go of your Egypt.
God will supply your every need.

A CRY AT MIDNIGHT

Have you ever been depressed
And had a broken heart,
So much tribulation
You didn't know where to start?

Have you been imprisoned
With suicidal thoughts,
Nothing seemed to work
And you couldn't pray as you ought?

Remember Paul and Silas
Who were cast in the Philippine jail
No pillow to rest their heads,
No way to pay their bail.

Can you see them standing there?
See the look on each face
Handcuffed and shackled
In such an awful place?

One began to sing.
The other began to pray.
A cry went up at midnight
For the Lord to have His way.

Their cries went up to heaven.
Their honest praises were heard.
They got the Father's attention.
Though He spoke not one word.

Their midnight cries touched His heart.
Suddenly the jail began to shake.
The place started to tremble
And the prisoners did awake.

The jail doors flew opened.
Bands were loosed from Paul and Silas' hands.
The jail keeper drew his sword
Because he didn't understand

That their cry at midnight
Which had been sent up to God
Had caused the jail to shake—
Had moved the Father's heart.

Have *you* ever tossed and turned
And could not sleep,
Your burden was so heavy
That you began to weep?

You too prayed at midnight.
You cried from the depth of your heart.
Your supplication was sent.
You sent it up to God.

And He opened the doors of heaven
To let your cry come in.
He heard your midnight cry
And gave you peace again.

YOU'LL NEVER RISE ABOVE
YOUR THOUGHTS

Where your thoughts are,
So is your heart.
Where your mind leads,
There your feet will trod.

Whatsoever things are lovely
Whatsoever things are true,
Should be the thoughts
That compel you

To walk each day in beauty,
And speak words of purity.
Your thoughts will bring you
To peace and security.

If you wish to succeed
Control what goes through your mind.
Low and defeatist thoughts
Will bring disaster every time.

Clear your head of cobwebs.
Stop reading and watching mess.
Filth in and garbage out
Never spell success.

Success begins from within
Your heart and your head.
Think on things of good report
Is what the Word said.

You are made to be a conqueror–
The head and not the tail.
A child of God is destined
To succeed and not to fail.

Study the Word; seek your gifts–
Benefits that Jesus' blood bought.
Keep repeating over and over:
"I'll never rise above my thoughts."

Shake off the thoughts of evil:
I'm not capable; I don't fit.
The world has much to offer.
Don't wait—- go out and take it.

You are what Jesus says you are.
He is your source and supply.
He wants you to trust in him,
Have faith, get up and try.

Jesus' blood paid the price.
Your success with his blood he bought.
Keep this on your mind
Because you'll never rise above your thoughts.

NEVER AGAIN

Some may wonder why I'm so happy–
Why I have not fallen apart.
It's because I have the love of Jesus
Flowing smack dab through my heart.

Others my ask, "Who is Jesus?
His worth we can not see."
This Jesus is my informer
Who made a believer out of me.

What is so special about him?
It is strange that you should ask.
He is a great Director.
He maps out my path.

If you would like to know him
Invite him to sup with you.
If he ever sits at your table
You'll learn what he can do.

Why not get to know him.
Let him tell you who *you are.*
No longer will you feel the need
To copy from some movie star.

He'll make you feel secure
And get rid of your low self-esteem.
After he dines at your table
I guarantee you'll be redeemed.

You'll become a new person.
No more will you suffer lack.
You may still have trials and tribulations
But they will not hold you back.

You'll be so glad you met him
And he has become your friend
Who'll be with you when times are rough,
Who'll stick through thick and thin.

So go on and invite him to visit–
Visit you in your home.
He'll be your life long companion.
Never again will you walk alone.

AT THE CROSSROAD

Standing at the crossroad
Feeling the wind blow
Searching from within,
Trying to figure which way to go.

Today is the day of decision
I can't remain at the crossroad.
I have a choice to make.
I need help to carry my load.

This decision must be mine.
No one can choose for me.
I am the responsible party.
Only I can walk out my destiny.

Nothing can be accomplished
While I stand here with indecision
Whether it will be God
Or the world and false religion.

The way is before me.
Today I must make a choice
To stand here at the crossroad
Or heed our Father's voice

To choose ye this day
The path I want to walk,
Whether to go with the truth
Or to continue to balk

And not take the road to Jesus,
The one who is in control.
The only road I can take
That has peace for my soul.

I can not remain here.
No longer can I stay.
I think I'll choose the cross.
There is no other way.

My decision is "Yes, Lord.
You are the tried and true.
On this road of life
I will follow you".

CLIMB

Why drown in your yesterdays?
Why wallow in your sorrows?
Why allow your yesterdays
To mess up your tomorrows?

You are not a victim
Of what you've been through.
Your past experiences
Were to prosper and bless you.

Change often hurts
And causes you to ache.
But you must to something different
For any progress you make.

Nothing new will take place
If you keep doing the same old thing.
So try something new
If you want your life to change.

This is a new season.
This season please embrace.
You have the power–
Strength to run life's race.

Keep practicing every day.
Old habits should not be repeated.
The race is not over.
You have not been defeated.

Why have a losing mentality?
This way of thinking must stop.
Rise up from the bottom.
Climb! Climb! Propel yourself to the top!

WALK TOWARD JORDAN

When your heart gets heavy
And about to weigh you down,
You call for your friends
Not a one can be found.

You can depend on Jesus.
He'll be there for you.
Just ask for his wisdom.
He will direct you.

If you are broke
And your bills are due,
Give them to Jesus
Let him pay them for you.

Your body may be feeble
You maybe cripple or lame.
People are scandalizing you
And calling you bad names.

Give your problems to Jesus.
Put them all in his hands.
He knows how you are hurting.
He already understands.

Don't turn to your neighbor
Who lives across the street.
He too is burdened–
Has shackles on his feet.

But God is unlimited.
He has no limits at all.
He is mightier than any mountain
It matters not how tall.

All the sand in the world
Are like a few pebbles at sea.
He is high; he is low.
He's anywhere he needs to be.

We can go to him in honesty.
We can go to him in prayer.
We can keep walking toward Jordan
And know he'll meet us there.

Though our Jordan may be deep
Our Jordan may be wide.
We can always depend on Jesus
To take us to the other side.

I AM WOMAN

I am
Caring, confident, compassionate,
Give me your support, your empathy,
And even your sympathy.

Take your pity.
Bury it deep, deep beneath the clay.
Shield me with your love. I can take
Charge.

I am
Brilliant, imaginative, witty, fun loving;
Housewife, mother, social worker, listener,
Career person, companion, stockbroker, a
Computer analyst all in one.

I can
Become absorbed in a book, enjoy sports,
Drive a race car, be a weight lifter or
A weight watcher.

I am daring.
I can fly the blue skies or sail the seven seas,
Dive the depths of the ocean or bathe
In the sun on the sunny shores.

I am
Sensual, tender, strong and shrewd if need be.
I want to be needed, never needy.

I am
Well educated and intellectually beautiful.

I am
Anything I choose to be.
Admire my tenacity. Accept my completeness.
Respect me for who I am. I am Black.

I am
Woman.

ARMED AND DANGEROUS

I 'm armed and dangerous.
Don't you mess with me.
The armor of God
Is my security.

I'm armed and dangerous.
Jesus is my big brother
Though I have an earthly father
And an earthly mother.

I'm armed and dangerous.
Faith is my shield.
When I put faith to use
Doubt has to disappear.

I am armed and dangerous.
On my feet I wear peace.
While traveling life's journey
Confusion must cease.

I am armed and dangerous.
Salvation protects my head.
As long as I wear the armor of God
I will never be afraid.

For he has given me protection
From my head to my feet,
In my home, on the road,
And on the dangerous streets.

I am armed and dangerous.
The spirit is my sword.
When the devil tries to attack me
I pierce him with the word.

YOUR SHIP IS ABOUT TO SAIL

Though your face is in the dust
You are able to breathe.
Arch your back.
Get up on your knees.

Then carefully erect yourself.
Stand on your feet– stand tall.
Build on hope; have faith.
Don't let yourself fall.

Step aboard the ship awaiting you.
Let the wind guide your sail.
Keep rowing down the river.
Cast out the word *fail*.

Steer your ship with courage.
Row close to the shore.
Don't be afraid to disembark.
From your experiences grow

Into a better person.
Have a brighter view
Of what life is all about—
The best path for you

To take for your future,
Your purpose for being here,
Which ship to board next
The reason you should not fear

To sail the mighty waters
Or navigate life seas.
Sail through the wind
And enjoy the cool breeze.

Tomorrow is a challenge.
But the Father won't let you fail.
Don't be shy; be relentless.
Aboard your ship and let it sail!

A LOST IS NOT A DEFEAT

During life's struggles
There will be troubled days.
Your path will sometimes crook
And turn all sort of ways.

At times you'll travel up hill.
Then you'll travel a normal road.
Other times you'll walk through valleys
Weighted down with a heavy load.

Some games you'll play and lose.
Other games you'll play and win.
There are times you'll fall on rocks
And end up with a bruised chin.

But get up and keep trying.
Never quit and throw up your hands.
It takes bruises and bumps
To grow into a woman or a man.

Yes, you'll lose many times
But there is something you *must* understand.
No lost ends up in defeat
If you do the best you can.

Think of your struggle as a lesson in life.
Take your bruises and bumps in stride.
Play each game the best you can.
Then walk off the court with pride.

Know that there is something within you.
There is the Power who controls.
Your lost is not a defeat
But a lesson more precious than gold.

Don't kick yourself
When you do the best you can.
Learn from every lesson.
Do the best you can.

A lost is a part of your experiences.
It is part of life's plan.
A lost is not ever a defeat.
It is becoming a woman or a man.

THINK IT OVER

Life is a bed of roses.
It's easy to fortune and fame.
People don't deliberately harm you,
Just to ruin your good name.

You can't lose your way
By following someone's tips.
You can't be misunderstood
By the way you move your hips.

You can fail to meet your destination
If you make the wrong turn.
It is very easy
To spend more than you earn.

You can accomplish the same thing
Though you don't do your best.
You can beat the odds
When you don't prepare for the test.

It does not matter
Who you pick for a friend.
No matter what the price
Right will always win.

You can get a good job.
It matters not how you look.
You can make it big
If you never read a book.

Good things always come
To those who wait.
Just by reading the Bible
You can make it through the pearly gates.

A person can do wrong
And never think twice.
Speak what comes to mind
Without paying a price.

It is a true fact
A mind is a terrible thing to waste.
Things are often done wrong
When they are done in haste.

If you have not taken time
To ponder over these thoughts
My advice to you:
"It's best you ought".

BE THE BEST YOU CAN

In today's time of fun and folly
We tend to forget
That even during this modern age
Some basic standards must be met.

Our way of doing and acting
Should follow the laws of God.
Keeping the body fresh and clean
Is where each of us can start.

Fads and fashion are costly.
They fade with each passing day.
Then you are left with fancy clothes
Only to throw them away.

So wear clothes that are becoming.
Keep your pants above your butt.
Wear a belt around your waste
To help hold them up.

Choose your words discreetly.
Watch how loudly you talk.
Be careful how you look.
Mind the way you walk.

There are times to be quiet.
Sometimes it's all right to be loud.
When you come into the house of God
Leave the noise outside.

Think before you act.
Honor your father and your mother.
Stand up for what is good.
Be careful how you treat one another.

Remember to say, "thank you".
Always be polite.
Don't forget to say, "please".
Walk away from those who fight.

Set your own standards
By the Golden Rule,
Never follow the crowd
Trying to be cool.

Think for yourself.
Keep your thoughts clean.
Did you know that bad behavior
Could prevent you from reaching your dream?

(Continued)

When you sit at the Father's table
Thank Him for your food.
Chew with your mouth closed
Not like a cow chewing its cud.

Wherever you happen to go
Be mindful of what you say and do.
Wherever you maybe;
Someone is always watching you.

So be sure to use good manners.
Take responsibility for yourself.
When things go wrong, as they sometimes do.
You're to blame and nobody else.

Set your standards high.
Work hard to see them through.
You can be successful.
Just ask God to see you through.

What I am trying to say is simple.
It should be plain and clear.
God expects you to do your best,
That is why He put you here.

GIVE IT ALL TO JESUS

Give it all to Jesus.
The battle belongs to him.
Stop holding on to your past
From which your hurts stem.

Give Jesus your disappointments.
Give him your hurts from yesteryear.
Leave them at the foot of the cross
Where they can disappear.

Let go of all your guilt.
Let go of the storms on your sea.
Allow Jesus to anchor your ship.
Allow him to set you free.

Let him put your skeletons in a coffin.
Let his love seal the lid down.
Give him your trials and tribulations.
He'll bury them in the ground.

Jesus will never dig them up
And give them to you again.
His blood is sufficient
To cover any kind of sin.

Give it all to Jesus.
He knows just what to do.
Give him your fears, your everything.
He died to redeem you.

KEEP YOUR FOCUS

This world we live in
Is filled with bumps and curves.
This has a tendency to
Wreck havoc on our nerves.

Though we say it is the world,
It is the people who inflict pain.
They go around gossiping
And give you a bad name.

If they see someone climbing
The ladder by leaps and bounds
Instead of pushing him up
They'll deliberately pull him down.

They put rocks in others paths
And tell a pack of lies.
I wonder if they know
That these things God despises.

If you ever find yourself
In a situation such as this
Keep your focus.
Retaliation you must resist.

If you are being lied on
Hold up your bruised chin.
A lie travels fast,
But the truth will win.

He who runs ahead
And put stones in another's path
May get noticed,
But the victim gets the last laugh.

Don't let outside interference
Give you the hocus-pocus.
Keep your eyes on your goal
And never lose your focus.

CHECK OUT YOUR MIND

Who told you that your brains are defected?
The truth is you are just fine.
Get a grip on yourself.
Check out your own mind.

So what if you've tried before
And you did not win.
Chalk it up to experience.
Go back and try again.

He who quits because of obstacles
Can never expect to win.
Success will come eventually.
Go back; give *try* another spin.

Clear your head of pass failures
And all the put-downs.
Get off of sinking sand.
Set your feet on solid grounds.

Whatever you spend your time doing,
Wherever your thoughts roam
Will determine your destiny—
Determine your place called home.

Work at something worth your while
And will not keep you entwined.
Never entertain negative thoughts.
Clear them from your mind.

Put your best foot forward
In everything you do.
Give your best at all times
And expect the best to return to you.

Don't hamper your progress
And continue to lag behind.
Get a move on yourself.
Check out your mind.

DON'T GIVE UP

Don't give up.
Don't despair.
Help the disadvantaged
Because you care.

Instead of cursing,
Say a little prayer.
Keep the faith.
Hang on in there.

Do a good job
Wherever you can.
Depend on God,
Not on man.

He is your strength.
He is the One to please.
Continue to be positive.
Roll up your sleeves.

He has kept you through danger
Seen and unaware.
Your guarding angels
Are everywhere.

Begin each day
With thanks to God.
Look to Him
For your just reward.

Your future is not
In the hands of man.
Pray for each other.
Do the best you can.

Right now you are struggling
With discouragement and pain.
God has kept you once.
Trust him to do it again.

It looks dark and bleak
And your nerves are worn.
Weeping endures for a night,
But joy comes in the morn.

Don't abandon your vessel.
Stay aboard; safeguard the crew.
Don't you know that our Father
Is watching over you?

Why worry about getting
That so called *pink slip.*
Your Father has you covered.
He is controlling your ship.

(Continued)

If one door is closed
He'll open another.
Lean on him.
Hang on my brother.

Put a smile on your face.
Don't worry or be afraid.
Refuse to become discouraged.
There is a brighter day ahead.

Behind every dark cloud
The sun always shines through.
Don't give up.
God has an answer for you.

Keep your eyes wide open.
Keep a listening ear
So when he speaks
You can clearly hear

What he is saying
And what he wants you to do.
He has a solution.
He has already made plans for you.

So don't grow weary.
Do the best you can.
Look to the hills for your help.
Put your future in the Potter's hand.

COME LORD

Come into my heart, Lord.
Let your love flow through.
Remove the film from my eyes.
Give me a clear view

So I can see my own faults
Instead of faults of my fellowman.
Give me a willing heart
To praise you as long as I can.

Come into my heart, Lord.
Take my guilt and stain away.
Then I can walk the narrow path
And from the broad road stray.

If you come into my heart
I'll have no room for hate.
When you open the doors of heaven
I will not hesitate

To march up to the door
And walk right on through
And receive my resting-place
Eternally home with you.

IT AIN'T OVER YET

The race has just begun.
The starting line is set.
Don't give in to your circumstances,
It ain't over yet.

Are your children going astray
And you don't know what to do?
No one seems to notice.
They don't even have a clue

That you are fighting
The biggest battle of your life.
The referee is shaking his head.
You've been knocked down twice.

You've tried to talk to your friends
But they are frustrated too.
You ask them for advice
But they can't answer you.

Now is your time
To get a grip on yourself.
Put your best foot forward
While you have time left.

Get up and start moving.
Hold up your chin.
The race is not over.
You have a chance to win.

Set your ship in motion.
Get ready to sail.
You are a go-getter.
Who said you have to fail?

Count all your blessings.
Be thankful for what you've got.
Don't become discouraged
Because you hit a rough spot.

From day one you were equipped
With tools for success.
Don't give up before you get started.
It is not your time to rest.

You have brains
And power you have never used.
You have a perfect generator.
Why let problems blow your fuse?

(Continued)

55

You can make it my child.
Don't you dare to fret!
Fight, strive, and keep on pushing!
It ain't over yet.

Your name has not been called.
You have not answered to the roll.
Stick out your chest.
Let your arms unfold

To all that is within you.
Use what's in your reach.
Learn all you can
From those who dare to teach.

Stand up to those
Who give you no respect.
The answer is forthcoming.
It ain't over yet.

You can be whatever you choose.
Don't complain; don't fret.
Keep climbing, my child.
It ain't over yet!

DIFFERENT OR SAME

Mexican, Haitian, Jews, Black or White
All are precious in His sight.
Each has a heart beating in his chest,
May get an attitude when under stress.

All people have blood that bleeds red,
Two eyes, a nose and one round head.
They want love and comfort in their home.
They feel uneasy when their children are gone.

They need food on their table and clothes to wear,
Shoes to put on when their feet are bare.
It matters not what your race, creed or color,
You need to co-exist and trust each other.

Read past history, then you can see
All human beings want to be free.
When you look at the picture, the facts are plain.
We are not that different, but very much the same.

WHO I AM

Who am I?
Is a question you may ask yourself.
What would I do
If I were broke with nothing left?

Would this make me a nobody
Who has no self worth?
Would this qualify me as a shadow
Who just appears here on earth?

I'll tell you *WHO I AM*
And who I am destined to be,
What I believe
And the things that control me.

To the world I am just a person–
A woman of the Black race.
Who is here by chance
Having no significant place.

What I do is depended on luck.
I am not supposed to be free–
Just a doomed ship
Drifting out on a mighty sea.

But the world has lied.
And misrepresented the truth.
Because I am someone special–
Have been since my youth

I got on board in April
Nineteen hundred forty-seven.
I am on a journey.
My destination is heaven.

I am a child of God.
He gave me a new name.
I am hooked up with Jesus.
No longer am I the same.

I have a father who loves me
To the core of my being.
He protects me from harm,
Dangers seen and unseen.

I am the head and not the tail.
I can fight the good fight
Because Jesus is my armor bearer
Who fights for me day and night.

I can speak to my mountains
And they will fall into the sea.
I have awesome power.
I have authority

(Continued)

To cast out
To loose and to bind
If only I keep the faith,
Let the Savior control my mind.

Though I have very little money
To call my own
I am rich; I am wealthy.
I have a comfortable home.

Since my father is King
He's in control of all the wealth.
In fact, everything there is
Belongs to him and no one else.

He has all the medicine
To heal any disease.
He owns enough tranquilizers
To put my mind at ease.

He controls the wind
That sets off the storms at sea.
To every bank in the world
My Father holds the keys.

He is in charge of the food
In every grocery store.
When supplies get low
He will order more.

He can stop my enemies
Dead in their tracks.
He has all the shoes I need
And clothes to cover my back.

All the things belong to my Father–
The things in heaven and on earth.
I became his child
By way of second birth.

So I am somebody–
The best there is.
Because he is mine.
Thank God I am his.

I can have what he says I can.
I can do what he says I can do.
My orders come from him
Not from the world or you.

I am a princess among princesses.
I am blessed beyond compare.
I can speak his name.
I can call him anywhere.

I am beautiful and wonderfully made.
I have been inducted in the Hall of Fame.
The president voted me in;
And Jesus is his name!

MYSTERY OF LIFE

Who of you can cast a stone;
Point a finger when you're alone
Or say what you'll do when all hopes are gone?
Neither you nor I.

Do you know the feeling of despair?
When you are going and getting nowhere,
And no one seems to care?
I do.

Do you know what it's like to be in pain,
Unpleasant thoughts about to drive you insane,
Unhappy events occur again and again?
I've been there.

Do you know what it's like to be confused,
Feel unwanted and emotionally abused,
Disrespected and singing the blues?
I know.

The fact is what goes up must come down.
What is passed comes back around,
And things that are lost sometimes are found.
Reality.

He who sows must also reap.
He who rejoices at times shall weep;
Sometimes tosses and cannot sleep.
Life's woes.

In the midst of all fear
There is one who is dear.
He is always standing near.
It's true.

He will always hold your hand,
Give you wisdom to understand,
And a home in the Promised Land.
He will.

TWO POINTS OF VIEW

By chance two strangers met
On top of a steep hill.
One kept fidgeting around
While the other one stood still.

"Here we are," said one stranger.
"Way up here alone.
It would have been much better
If we both had stayed home."

"What better off
Would you and I be
If we were back home with others
Unable to be free?"

"At least there'd be a few friends
Who'd probably wish us well.
Being on top of this lonely hill
Is no worst than being in hell.

I came up here
Because I was full of myself.
I got sick and tired of
Helping everybody else."

The other stranger said nothing
While gazed at the sun of gold.
Breaking his silence he exclaimed,
"What beauty to behold!

Being on top of this hill
Gives me a chance to see
That God in his great wisdom
Made hills for serenity.

Here I can be at peace
And enjoy the sights on earth.
I can feel the holy presence
Of the creator of the universe."

"How can you experience peace
Where there is no fuss,
No cars, no stores, no anything
But just the two of us?

I'd be much better off
If I could talk on the phone.
Being up here with you
Is *far* worse than being at home."

Said the other stranger,
"I can hear someone calling my name.
I can hear melodious voices.
Oh what beautiful songs they sang!

Another voice is whispering,
'My child, I welcome you here
To spend some time with me
In an holy atmosphere.'

(Continued)

Over there I can see my Maker
In the form of green trees.
I feel him in the air
He caresses me with the breeze.

There is his smile
In the twinkling of the sun.
I would not have been this sensitive
Had I remained at home."

The first stranger spoke to the other,
"You can stay here and talk and talk.
But I am getting off this hill.
I only wish I didn't have to walk.

There were many folks
I stepped over way downhill.
Climbing up here was fine.
Going down is not much a thrill.

You see I'll have to explain
Why my trip was cut short.
My efforts and my struggles
All have gone for naught."

Then the voice of wisdom spoke
As clearly as could be.
"What could be so wrong
if you two joined with me?

We could walk together
And cushion each other's fall.
If we work together
There may not be a crash at all.

We wouldn't have to worry
About what the world may ask.
They could readily see
We walked the same path.

A path some call freedom.
Others call it eternity.
It matters not what they call it.
It is the road for me."

Finally, the disgruntle stranger
Smiled and nodded his head.
He must have had a change of heart
Because these of the words he said:

"What a great revelation
That I met you my brother.
Now I know what it means
To help one another.

I too have met the Creator
On top of this lonely hill.
Had I not met you up here
I'd be complaining still.

I am so glad you introduced me
To the creator of the sun.
Thank you for showing me
I don't have to walk alone."

PRESS ON

Press through!
You are on your way out.
Press on!
Never let yourself doubt.

The Lord is your strength.
He is your refuge.
Press! my child.
There is an answer for you.

Don't you dare stop!
Don't you dare turn around!
Plant your feet.
Plant them on solid ground.

Your footing is sure.
Your hope is in Him.
Press on my child.
Though the way looks dim.

He has promised
To watch your back.
Press on!
In him there is no lack.

When you don't know what to do
Praise him! Look up.
Praise the only one
Who is filling your cup.

He will give you strength.
He will give you power.
He'll stand by you
Every minute...every hour.

So press on my child.
Press your way through.
Trust in God Almighty.
Who is to say what you can not do?

His word is your security blanket.
You are safe in his arms.
Press on!
Nothing can do you harm.

Don't stop pressing until the race is over.
Stop wandering around in the wilderness.
Press on! Press on!
In him there is success!

DON'T LISTEN

Do not listen to old Satan.
I know he's hanging around
Trying to steal your glory
And mess with your heart and mind.

He's a liar; don't believe him.
You know what God has done.
Tell him, "Get out of my way.
I believe in God's only son."

Don't become discouraged
If you have not find a job to do.
Keep the faith; take heart in knowing
That God is looking out for you.

Right now it may look bleak.
It maybe a struggle trying to pass.
Don't sweat the small stuff.
Take Jesus to your class.

Trust Him with all your heart.
To your own understanding lean not.
In all you do put him first.
He gave you everything you've got.

Turn it all over to Him.
Give Him your job, life, and test.
Look to the hills from whence come your help.
In the Savior is your success.

Don't entertain negative thoughts.
They send your faith out yonder.
Tell **IT**, "Get out my way.
You'll never steal my thunder."

In all things do your best.
Praise God; give Him the glory.
Look from where you've come.
Your life is a living story!

DREAM ON BLACK MAN

Dream on Black man.
Now don't you stop.
Keep climbing Black man
Until you reach the top.

Look all around you.
Open your ears.
The clock is ticking.
Don't give in to your fears.

They'll try to deceive you
By giving you a number.
Work hard Black man.
Don't let them steal your thunder.

Let your presence be felt in the banks.
Get on the ball in the classrooms at school.
Learn all you can.
Don't be anybody's fool.

Keep on striving Black man.
You do your best.
You've got to be ready
To pass the test.

Know this my brother.
There isn't a battle that you can't win.
You've done it once.
Go do it again.

We need teachers to teach,
Lawyers to plead our case.
We need God fearing people
To preserve our race.

Dream on Black man.
Don't give up hope.
Be strong Black man.
Don't take that dope.

Take back your children.
Get them out of the street.
Dream on Black man.
Don't go down in defeat.

The doors have been opened,
But this I can't understand.
Why we kill each other
Then blame it on the other man.

(Continued)

73

Go back home with your family.
Take your children by the hand.
Stand tall Black brother.
Fill your shoes; be a man.

Take your family in the car,
And drive them to church.
Show them the way to God.
It doesn't cost very much.

Keep trusting in Him.
Never lose faith, my brother.
Things will get better
When we stop hurting each other.

Stand up to your responsibilities.
Stop blaming the White man.
The sky is the limit.
What is your plan?

You can prepare yourself
To walk in the opened door.
Or you can do nothing
And hurt more and more.

Take up the cause
For which King and others fought.
We are enjoying the freedom
With their lives, it was bought.

Catch hold to the plow.
Don't you ever turn back.
Our children need you.
This is a proven fact.

Hold fast Black brother
To what is yours.
Strive on Black man
Keep walking through the doors.

Show the world
That you demand respect.
Straighten up my brothers.
Earn your paycheck.

Wake up Black man.
Open your eyes.
Don't let them fool you.
Keep your eyes on the prize.

Dream on Black man.
Now don't you stop.
Keep climbing Black man
Until you reach the top.

GET YOUR BACK OFF THE WALL

Take your face out of the dirt.
You still have enough air to breathe.
You can arch your back
And get up on your knees.

Push! Stand tall!
Build on your hope.
Get your back off the wall!

Hold tightly to life's ship.
Let his power navigate your sail.
Keep rowing toward the shore
Knowing that you can not fail.

Believe that you have the power
To overcome obstacles great or small.
Why be hesitant.
Get your back off the wall!

Don't keep shuffling your feet
And keep looking down!
Hold up your head.
How dare you wear a frown!

You are special!
More precious than gold!
Get away from the wall!
You take control!

The wall is at your back.
So focus on what is ahead.
Walk away! Be strong!
Don't be afraid!

Use the gifts you have.
So what, if you stumble and fall.
Pick yourself up! Try again!
Get your back off the wall!

There is no need to hide behind it.
The wall is there to block your view,
To keep you from seeing
The things meant for you.

Get on the move!
Meet your destiny–your call.
Begin today! Success is yours!
Now get your back off the wall!

HANG ON TO HOPE

When the trials of daily life
Give you negative vibes
Hang on to HOPE.
Push negativism aside.

If it seems impossible
Accept possible; leave off *im.*
Tighten up your loins.
Hang on with vigor and vim.

Never dwell on past failures
Nor yesterday's pain.
Hang on to HOPE.
Bounce back and try again.

Let your defeats be steppingstones
Instead of blunders.
Hang on to HOPE.
Let it keep you from going under.

Yesterday's battle is over.
Each day is a new beginning.
The battle maybe lost,
But the war you are winning.

The victory does not go to the quitter.
It goes to the one who does his best.
So hang on to HOPE.
It is the first step to success.

Hope is the key.
It lets you inside.
You can not win doing nothing
Or looking for a free ride.

HOPE puts you in touch
With your inner self.
Hang on to HOPE
When there's nothing left.

Don't give up.
Fight the good fight.
Hang on to HOPE.
Hang with all your might.

On success
Never put a seal.
Hang on to HOPE
As long as you live.

The banner goes to the one
Who thinks he can.
HOPE gives you strength.
HOPE enables you to stand.

HELP IS ON THE WAY

Sister, don't give up.
Don't despair.
Keep thanking and praising him.
I know he really cares.

So never, ever doubt him.
Don't whine or complain.
Lay hold of his promises.
Take hold in Jesus' name.

Today maybe hard.
The future may look bleak.
Just keep trusting him
His will daily seek.

His word is your hope.
His word is true.
He promised many years ago
To take care of you.

Hold up your head.
Put a smile on your face.
Don't you know
God has given you a place?

He knows all your hurts,
Your needs, and your pain.
Look to him; accept his promises.
Do it all in Jesus' name.

He has your number.
He knows where you stay.
Cheer up my sister.
Help is on the way!

ONCE AGAIN

Once again I thank you
For a brand new day.
Let me start it with you
And do things your way.

Enable me to rejoice
In everything I say and do.
Keep my thought clean and pure.
Keep my mind stayed on you.

When this day is over
I want to have done my best
To give you thanks and praises
So I can have a peaceful rest,

Sleep softly like a baby,
Slumber without fear,
Without a confused mind,
Because you are standing near.

To keep me and protect me
Under your watchful eye.
Hold me in your precious arms
And sing me a lullaby

Saying, "Rest my child.
Have a good night.
I like what you did today.
You honored me just right!"

JESUS IS BIGGER THAN YOUR STORM

Into each life
The wind will blow.
From whence it comes
You'll never know.

Sometimes the wind
Will change to a storm.
Thunder and lightning
Threaten to do you harm.

Is there a storm
Blowing in your life today—
A storm so big
It's getting hard to pray?

Search yourself
And the position you're in.
Is your storm
The results of sin?

Is there some person
You need to forgive?
Do you need to make changes
In the way you live?

Perhaps your storm
Is a lesson being taught,
A bat being swung
Or a ball not caught.

Jesus is bigger
Than a storm you go through.
He is your savior.
He died for you.

Speak to your storm
That is hammering your head.
Tell your storm
What God almighty said.

Though you walk through the valley
Of trouble and despair
Don't be discouraged
Your deliverer is there.

Hold on to his word.
Never allow yourself to doubt.
Trust in him.
He will bring you out.

Neither hell nor high waters
Can hold you back.
Your Savior has everything.
Nothing does he lack.

Storms come in your life
For unknown reasons
Don't become weary.
They only last for a season.

(Continued)

Wait out your storm
Hold your peace.
Wait out your storm.
Tell the wind to cease.

So don't let your storm label you
Nor define who you are.
Press your way through.
Come out like a star.

Make Jesus the eye of the storm
That comes your way.
If Jesus is the center
No storm can stay.

Hold on to his hand
While cleaning up debris.
The battle belongs to Jesus
You got the victory.

He is your deliverer.
Stay secure in his arm,
Give it all to Jesus.
He is bigger than your storm.

GOD LOVES YOU

God loves you
Not because you are a movie star.
Nor because you're so grand.
He loves you because of who you are.

You were made in his image.
Just the way he wanted you to be.
His love for you
Caused him to die on the tree.

He says,"Come unto me.
Bring your hurts and your pains.
Bring your sick bodies
I'll make them well again.

Bring me your disappointments,
Your shortcomings and your lacks.
Don't look behind you.
I have your back.

Give me what is bothering you.
Come to me in prayer.
Lay your concerns on the altar.
Leave all your troubles there.

It does not matter where you've been
Nor the things you use to do.
I am your heavenly Father.
You are my child; I love you".

HOLD FAST

Hold fast to your dreams.
Let them grow and grow.
Dreams are the first steps
To places you wish to go.

Your world is as big as you make it.
Life is lived one day at a time.
You can never stand up
If you keep sitting down.

Get up and start trying.
Your future is in your hand.
Nothing is ever achieved by wishing,
But by doing what you can.

Don't be afraid to take a chance,
Or try something new.
Change does not come
If you keep doing what you use to do.

Get out of your comfort zone.
Launch out into the deep.
Your ship can't sail in shallow water.
Nothing is accomplished while you sleep.

Roll up your sleeves and push.
Get a new lease on life.
Start through the door of success.
Push; don't look back twice.

Play by the rules each day.
Strive to be all you can.
Life will soon pass you by
Unless you have a vision and a plan.

Think big.
Stand tall as a Georgia pine.
Little can you accomplish
If you don't renew your mind.

Tell yourself you can.
Tell yourself you will.
You don't belong in the valley.
Your place is at the top of the hill.

Hold fast to your dreams.
Hold fast to your desire.
Goals are not reached by wishing.
They are reached by those who try.

Don't become discouraged.
Don't stand and hold your hands.
Go after what you want in life.
You have the power; I know you can.

IT IS IN HIS HANDS

Thousands may fall about you
And ten thousands at your side.
No weapon formed against you shall prosper
If the Savior is thy guide.

Instead of fuming
Say a little prayer.
Keep the faith.
Hang on in there.

Do the best you can do.
Don't depend on man.
Put your trust in God.
Your life is in his hand.

He is your strength.
He is the one to please.
Always be positive.
Roll up your sleeves.

He has brought you through
Danger seen and unaware.
Your guarding angels
Are stationed everywhere.

Begin each day
With thanksgiving to God.
Look to him
For your just reward.

Let him be the rock
On which you stand.
Cast your cares on him.
Put them all in his hands.

If you are struggling
With heartache and with pain.
Turn it over to the Doctor.
It is all in his hand.

If one door closes
Look to God; he'll open another.
Pray for yourself,
Your sister and your brother.

The sun has gone down.
You're standing on sinking sand.
Have faith in God.
You are in the Potter's hand.

(Continued)

Don't abandon the ship.
Stay on board with the crew.
Take heart.
The Father cares for you.

Put a smile on your face.
Don't be afraid.
Refuse to become discouraged.
There are brighter days ahead.

Behind every cloud
The sun comes through.
Don't give up!
God has an answer for you.

Keep your eyes opened
And maintain a listening ear.
So when he calls
You can clearly hear

What he is saying,
What he wants you to do.
Tune in to his bidding.
He has thought it through.

So stop whining and complaining.
Do the very best you can.
Never worry about the future.
THE FUTURE IS IN GOD'S HAND1

GO ON

Don't allow the enemy
To put his monkey on your back,
Stuff all his rubbish and junk
And overload your sack.

Then you drag it around with you
Day after day,
Weighed down with his stuff
And can hardly find your way.

There is no need to listen
And let him fill you with deceit;
When there is a stronger power within you
Keeping you on your feet.

Strut on to the river.
Let the Bridge carry you across.
Pick up your feet; increase your pace.
Jesus has paid the cost.

Work while you have momentum.
Work while you can grow.
There are things for you to do,
And places you must go.

Go on to another height.
Step with dignity.
Don't be discouraged or dismayed.
Go on and fight for victory!

IT'S ENOUGH

What you have in your arsenal
Is quiet sufficient for you
To be prosperous in life.
What you have will carry you through.

Your Creator gave you in the beginning
What you needed for the ride.
Whatever it takes for you
He will provide.

He knew you before you
Were conceived in your mother's womb.
He equipped you for an abundant life;
Not a life of doom.

For Moses it was a staff,
A cane he held in his hand.
All he had to do was to use it,
And follow God's command.

Whenever Moses listened
To what the Master said
He marched into victory.
Never once was he afraid.

He was called out of the desert
From among the fields.
Moses was sufficiently equipped
To do God's divine will.

Never concern yourself with
What has been given to another.
Just use what *you* have.
Don't depend on sister or brother.

Your gift may look small.
It may not seem grand.
But your gift is *your* fortune.
Just follow the potter's plan.

Cultivate your field
Though you have only a few feet.
Your territory is big enough
To make your harvest complete.

Plant your seeds
If it's in your own yard.
Don't worry about the outcome.
Your harvest is in the hands of God.

Never give up because the future looks hopeless
Or your days seem black as night.
Use what has been given to you.
Let the Savior create the light.

Your problems may seem insurmountable–
As big as the Red Sea.
God will part your waters
And drown your enemy.

So tap into the resources
He gave you in the beginning.
God has given you enough for a lifetime
To keep you forever winning.

LAY DOWN YOUR BURDENS

We are all on a journey
Though we travel a different road.
Each of us is struggling
With some kind of load.

Yes, we are carrying burdens.
Sometimes we have days of rain.
So much of this and that.
So many heartaches and pain.

One may be filled with loneliness
Thinking, *I have only me.*
Another is fighting a battle
With no sight of victory.

You may be burden with disappointment.
Your friend let you down
Now you walk around in a stupor
With your face turned toward the ground.

My burden could be poverty.
I can not pay my bills.
The person across the street is sick
No doctor can cure her ills.

A man down town carries unforgiveness
He can't even forgive himself.
His guilt is so heavy
He can think of no one else.

The person sitting behind you
Needs love and a trusting friend,
Anyone, anything to lean on,
A person on which to depend.

It does not matter who you are
Or what you're all about.
You are carrying a load–
A load you could do without.

Why keep struggling
With so much stuff?
Don't you know that you can't hang,
That you have carried it long enough?

(Continued)

Take all your junk to the cross.
Pour it out and leave it there,
Lay down your heavy burdens.
Go to God in prayer.

He'll take all you have.
It will not cost you a cent.
Lay down your burdens.
Go to him and repent.

Once you lay your burdens down
Walk away with a happy heart.
Don't look back in regret.
Leave your burdens with God.

He is capable.
He can handle anything.
Lay down your burdens.
Never pick them up again.

VOICE OF REASON

In the midst of idleness and silence of the night
I heard a voice whisper though the figure was not in sight.
"I am the voice of reason; I have advice for you.
Lend your ears for a few minutes then I'll be through.

If you want to be successful you must not procrastinate.
Dedicate yourself to the task at hand, prepare and participate."
Then Reason disappeared, but I remembered what she said.
The record still plays over and over in my head.

So when I have a task to do I never ever wait.
I remember the advice of reason "not procrastinate".
When others are frolicking, thinking they are having fun.
I don't neglect the job at hand; I work until the job is done.

HE LOVES YOU

Don't ever be discouraged.
Never ever despair.
Just keep on walking
'Cause you know God is there.

If men talk about you
And misused your name,
Take heart in knowing
That they did the Savior the same.

Look all around you.
Witness God's creation.
He gave His Son to the world
For our deliverance and salvation.

So there is no need to be afraid,
Neither blunder or get lost.
Just walk on to the river.
Jesus is there to help you across.

He's there waiting
With outstretched hands,
Saying, "come on home my child.
Receive your promised land.

It was created by My Father
A long time ago.
God sent Me in the flesh
Because He loves you so.

Just believe what is written.
Live by My Father's command.
Come on, child; don't you worry.
Close by your side He'll stand.

When dark clouds arise
And strong winds blow,
Keep trusting in My Father
Everywhere you go."

RISE UP

Rise up my sisters and brothers.
Don't let circumstance get you down.
So what if your mother have to work
And your daddy is not around?

Sometimes your stomach churns,
Aches, and growls for food.
There is nowhere to turn.
You live in a bad neighborhood.

People hang on the corners.
Dope pushers roam the streets.
There seems to be a problem
With everyone you meet.

Just last night you saw a shadow
Lurking in and out your home.
All you could do was tremble—
Too scared to cry, too hurt to groan.

You're afraid of the dark.
Yet you hate the light of day.
Rise up sister! Rise up brother!
There is hope; there is a way.

Start taking charge.
Build on what is left.
Speak to that inner voice.
Begin to encourage *yourself.*

You still have a chance.
The enemy hasn't taken you out.
Rise up sisters and brothers!
Never lose hope; don't you doubt.

Where there is a will
There is a way.
Be careful how you think.
Watch what you say.

You were made for a purpose.
You were created with what you need.
Your creator gave you all the qualities–
Everything it takes to succeed.

Stop thinking *failure.*
Get *that* thought out of your head.
Hold on to God's promises.
Take hold of what he said.

You were made in his image.
You were bought with a price.
You have the tools.
Go on, live a prosperous life.

Seize every opportunity.
Claim all your benefits.
Strive my sisters and my brothers!
Rise up! You can make it!

LET GO, LET GOD

Turn loose all your cares.
Put them in the Master's hand.
Let him be your rock–
The foundation on which you stand.

Give him your life.
It is his anyway.
He is the Creator
Of your birthday.

Give him your fears.
They were invented by the evil One
Who is trying to keep you
From letting God's will be done.

Let go your finances.
Give them back to the Creator.
Let go your mind.
Turn it over to the originator.

Let him have your children.
Put him in control.
He knows how to handle them.
He is the giver of their souls.

Don't even worry about their future.
Their future is already in his hand.
He knows how to lead them
He has a plan

For all of his children–
For each of his offspring.
Let go; let God.
He can handle anything.

Give him all you have–
Everything you think you own.
You're not able to handle it.
Why not leave it alone.

God knows all the ins and outs.
He knows what ails you.
Let go; let God.
He is your rescue.

YOU ARE SOMEBODY

Who told you
That you are nobody
Unless you are drinking
And throwing a wild party?

That you are destined to fail;
Or you have weak brains
Which cause you to do
Low down and evil things?

Or maybe you heard
That you have a low IQ.
Therefore you can not achieve
As well as others do.

Well, I got news for you.
There is not a word to it!
No validity, no truth,
Not even a little bit!

You were made in God's image;
A little lower than the angels.
You have his assurance that
He will protect you from dangers.

Though you are weak;
In him you are made strong.
His word is a guide.
It teaches you right from wrong.

Because you are a child of God
Believe that you can achieve.
Ask in faith for what you want.
Then act like you've already received.

On the day of conception
God had a destiny for you.
Don't let negative thoughts
Keep you from doing what you need to.

You are a child of God!
You are alive!
Shout it to the house top:
"I have arrived!

Don't you ever try to sell me short.
Don't try to take *my* joy away!
I am his; he is mine.
Under *his* guidance I shall forever stay!"

LET HIM TAKE CONTROL

Look at the face in the mirror.
Listen to your own heart.
Why listen to the critics?
Why let them tear you apart?

Who are they to tell you
What you are all about?
Do they know you
From inside out?

All the negative things you hear
Are most likely no good.
Never let them overtake your mind
And prevent you from doing what you should.

Block out failure.
Encourage yourself.
You are the determining factor.
You–no one else

Speak to the inner man.
Friend, open your eyes.
Take stock of yourself
And you'll be surprised

To know that you are special.
You are one of a kind.
Don't be confused.
Get a grip; control your mind.

Take an inventory of your being.
See what's in your soul.
Wake up! Don't be sluggish.
Be alert! Take control!

You can be what you want to be.
Hitch your wagon to a star.
No one knows your future.
Man can't define who you are.

He is not aware
Of what is going on with you.
Man can not decide
What you can or cannot do.

So dig deep down my child,
Deep down inside your soul.
Get it together!
God is in control.

(Continued)

You were made with a purpose.
So plan your destiny.
Purge out all the put-downs.
Relieve yourself of misery.

Go back; look in the mirror.
Do you see a loser or a winner?
Do you see a man of purpose
Or a great pretender?

The dawn of a new day
Is spreading over your face.
There is a twinkle in your eyes.
Defeatist thoughts have been replaced

With confidence, self-esteem
And a new attitude.
Never more listen to
"Child, you are no good."

You have power swelling up in you,
Raging like a roaring lion.
Look left and right.
Leave your failures behind.

What is there to hinder you
From being all you can be.
Get busy! Unlock the door.
You have the key.

Use it.
Use your brilliant mind.
Unlock the closed doors.
Unlock doors of all kind.

Strive! Let the adrenal flow.
Your success is about to unfold.
Step up! Get going!
Let the Savior take control.

LET IT BE

You have gotten comfortable
Even in your misery.
You desire change.
Yet you are afraid to be free.

While traveling this road
Perhaps you made a wrong turn.
Something you swallowed
Caused you heartburn.

A friend deceived you–
Let you fall to the ground.
Instead of lifting you up
He held you down.

So your parents did not want you.
Said, "you were a mistake."
Bringing you into this world
Caused their hearts to ache.

Your boss is unfair.
He didn't give you a promotion.
No one noticed the time you put in,
Your hard work and devotion.

You don't look like others.
Your eyes are crossed.
You still hurt
From the things you lost.

You have no known talent,
And a bald, shiny head,
Few clothes, a tiny piece of meat,
And a mighty little bread.

People talk about you
And treat you mean.
Your daddy is absent.
You have low self-esteem.

Perhaps many other things
Are a part of your past.
Be of good cheer!
These things won't last.

They were put in your path
To make you better.
Not to be a loser,
But a *go-getter!*

(Continued)

Nothing that has happened
Can be undone.
But it *can* determine
How well you run.

Use your experiences
To give you strength.
Change your stride.
Stretch out your length.

You'll never succeed
While holding yourself down.
You can't smile
If you're wearing a frown.

So get a new attitude.
Let go of your past.
Change your thinking.
Free yourself at last.

Change doesn't come easily.
The process is slow.
You can't get bigger
If you refuse to grow.

You can't move forward
While backing back.
Nor lighten your load
While stuffing your sack

With yesterdays failures
And yesterdays' pains,
Or counting your losses
And forgetting your gains.

The message my child
By now you should know:
You can't live in the past.
So turn it loose; let it go.

Then fly like an eagle.
You begin to soar.
Turn loose your past.
LET IT GO!

PAYDAY WILL COME

Be careful each day
Where you work or play.
How you work
Is what determines your pay.

If you go to the field
But do not plant any seeds.
There'll be no harvest—
Nothing to meet your needs.

So if you want a good harvest
You must go out and sow
Seeds of love and kindness.
Your harvest will begin to grow.

In fact, it will multiply
Far beyond what you expect.
Just keep on working.
Never fail or neglect

Those who are around
That are less fortune than yourself.
Give according to your blessings.
Never worry about what's left.

For if you help others
To meet their daily needs
God will abundantly reward you
For each and every deed.

However, if you sow seeds
Of spite and deceit
Your harvest will also multiply
With snares to tangle your feet.

Like David who stole
The poor man's wife;
Payday cost him
His firstborn's life.

So when you get your pay check
There should be no surprise—
Whether you'll be happy
Or walk away with teary eyes.

The bottom line is
Put in a good day's work my friend.
Then your reward will be happiness
And prosperity in the end.

If you have done your work
And your work was well done,
You'll have nothing to fear
When payday comes.

It will be profitable.
Adequate will be your pay.
Your countenance will be happy.
Not a word can you say.

'Tis best you do a good job
Whether you work night or day.
Then you won't be disappointed
When you stand before God for your pay.

TAKE A LOOK

What are the things
That are standing in your way?
What is holding you back
And messing up your day?

Does what others say about you
Haunt you day and night?
Do negative thoughts keep you
From putting up a good fight?

Are you listening to the words
"Man you are no good"?
Have what you've been through
Given you a bad attitude?

Does low self-esteem
Have you frozen in your tracks?
Are you letting the fear of failure
Hold you back?

Are you still hanging with the losers
Who never do their best;
Allowing their *don't care* attitudes
To block your own success?

If so, tell all the losers
To step aside.
Get on about your business.
Strive with faith and pride.

Let today be a new day
And begin the climb uphill.
You have places to go
And dreams to fulfill.

Don't let what you've been told
About what you can or can not do
Plant negative thoughts in your head.
Be positive and propel yourself through.

Nothing or anyone can stop you.
If you believe you can do well.
Study and stay focused.
There's no reason you have to fail.

You have been given what it takes—
Everything you need.
Remember, those who do their best
Are the ones who usually succeed.

THEN AND NOW

The history of the Black man
Started many years ago.
Some of the good he did
You and I will never know.

But let us talk about some
Of the successes he has had.
History was not completely erased.
Of this, I'm very glad.

Did you know that a Black man
Invented the first traffic light?
Crispus Attucks was the first to die
When he was sent on the front line to fight?

Fredrick Douglas and Harriet Tubman
Put their lives on the line.
Our people were led to freedom
With dogs following closely behind.

Benjamin Banneker
Invented a clock
By using his brains
And a few wooden blocks.

George Washington Carver
Find many uses for peanuts.
He used what he had.
There're no *ifs, ands,* or *buts.*

A Black woman who found a college
Was Mary McCloud Bethune.
Booker T. Washington worked his way through college
By sweeping floors with a broom.

Of course, Medgers evers
Was gunned down late at night
All because
He wanted his civil rights.

Shirley Chishom and Jesse Jackson
Ran for president of this nation.
They went through hardships,
Trials, and tribulations.

Dr. Martin Luther King
Went to jail and walked picket lines.
He kept pressing on
Until he was gunned down.

(Continued)

Dr. Carter G. Woodson
The truth about our history, he did seek.
He wrote several books
And started Black History Week.

Rosa Parks stood firmly
By not giving up her seat on the bus.
Her boldness and tenacity
Paved the way for all of us.

Not so many years ago
Hank Aaron broke the record by hitting 715 homeruns.
He stuck to the task.
He got the job done.

Mayo Angelo
Came through an awful situation.
Yet she kept moving along
And earned a good education.

There are other sisters and brothers
Black like you.
Their blackness didn't stop them
From doing what they could do.

There are so many more.
I could go on and on.
Some are still living.
Others have been called home.

But I have a question
I want to ask each of you.
They did their part.
What are you going to do?

You can make it
Against all odds.
All you have to do
Is trust in God.

Don't sit on the stool of do nothing
Complaining and waiting for a handout.
You have what it takes.
There is no doubt.

God gave each of you
A task to do.
Stop dragging your feet.
He's looking at you.

(Continued)

If you can't do one thing
Then do another.
You don't have to fight
And harm one another.

Take what you have
And put it to use.
There is no time to cry
Neglect and abuse.

Start today.
Develop your mind.
God gave you brains.
Why play around?

You've heard about many
Who have gone before and paved the way.
What are you doing?
What do you have to say?

I GIVE IT ALL TO YOU

I give it all to Jesus—
My sorrows and my tears.
Father, I give it all to you—
My hopes and my fears.

I give you all my concerns,
My family—the things they need to do.
I give it all to you, Savior.
Because you have brought me through.

I give you my body,
My aches, hurts and pain.
I give you my thoughts.
I give you everything.

I give you my enemies.
I give you those who put me down.
I give you the freedom
To think through my mind.

Come on in heavenly Father.
You take control.
I give you all.
I give you my soul.

YOU DON'T KNOW

Unless you've walked the distance in my shoes
And felt the intensity of my hurt,
Then you cannot begin to understand
Why I wear a torn shirt.

Can you honestly say,
"Nadene, I know how you feel"
When you've never drunk from my glass
Nor swallowed all my pills?

You may empathize with me.
Give your opinion if you must.
But when I'm crying in agony
Don't ask me to stop my fuss.

Only the Father knows where I am.
He knows what I carry on my back.
He knows the many things
That are filling up my sack.

Each of us has an order.
Each one has a part to play.
So don't go around gossiping
Talking about why I act this way.

Instead, help me to bear my burdens.
Help me to carry my load.
Smooth out the bumps and rough places
That are all over my road.

Do all you do for God's glory.
Then let the tare grow with the wheat.
Turn it over to the Master.
Don't try to sit in His seat.

Let your continence be pleasant.
Let you gossip and idle talk cease.
Judgement is never yours.
It belongs to the Prince of Peace.

Share what you have with others.
It is a loan from God to you.
Give without counting the cost
Is what he wants you to do.

Let the Savior be your focus.
To Him belongs the glory.
He gave us believers the Great Commission
To go out and tell the story.

YOU MADE IT!

You took everything in stride
And went about your way.
You had to decide
To have a graduation day.

Some thought you'd never make it——
To graduate from high school.
You proved them wrong.
Now who is the fool?

You hung in there.
You stood fast.
You kept on going.
Each test you passed.

Now high school is behind you.
But you must go on.
Your life is not over.
In fact, you've just begun.

So set yourself in motion.
Reach for the sky.
Anything is possible.
If you'll only try.

Don't let anyone sell you short
Nor mess with your mind.
Just know my child.
You are one of a kind.

Your next hill is steep.
No one can tell you what to do.
If you reach the top
It all depends on you.

So ask God for wisdom.
Ask Him to direct your path.
Do your best at all times.
This is all any of us can ask.

Hats off to you!
You are a winner; yes indeed!
With God as your pilot
You are destined to succeed.

WHO DO YOU SEE IN THE MIRROR?

Take a look at yourself in the mirror.
Do you feel what's in your heart?
Are you listening to the critics
And letting them tear you apart?

Who are they to tell you
What you are all about?
Do they know your true self?
Do they know you from inside out?

All the negative things they tell you
Are more than likely no good.
This is the plan of the enemy
To keep you from doing what you should.

Don't pay the blabbers any attention.
Start encouraging yourself.
You are the determining factor——
You, no one else.

Begin to talk to yourself.
Friend, open wide your eyes.
Take a good look in the mirror.
You will be surprised

To know that
You're one of a kind.
What are you telling yourself?
What is controlling your mind?

Have you ever taken an inventory
Of yourself–what is in your soul?
Throw out all the fear and doubt.
Wake up; take control.

You can be whatever you choose to be.
So reach for a star.
Never allow others to hedge you in.
Never let them determine who you are.

You are in control
Of what is going on.
You are the determining factor
You, and you alone.

Dig deep down my child.
Dig deep inside your soul.
Get it together; encourage yourself.
Let the Creator take control.

You were made for a purpose.
Take hold of your destiny.
Purge out all the put-downs.
Get rid of your misery.

Look once more in the mirror.
Stand there in the center.
Do you see a defeated wimp?
Or do you see a winner?

Can't you see victory
Lighting up your face?
Feel the adrenaline
Giving you power to run your race.

(Continued)

Feel the fresh energy
Swelling inside of you.
Flex your muscles.
Do what you have to do.

What is there to hinder you
From being what you want to be?
Get busy not tomorrow but today.
You have the key.

Use the key
To unlock the door of your mind.
Walk on in.
Close the door behind

To all the criticism
To self doubt and shame,
To anyone who is talking
And trying to ruin your name.

Remember whom you saw in the mirror.
It was the real you.
Not a self doubter,
But one who is secure

In her ability
To tackle any task at hand.
The person you saw in the mirror
Is the one who has a plan

To accomplish her goal,
To work until she's through.
You saw a *real* person in the mirror.
That real person is **YOU.**

SOAR ABOVE ADVERSITIES

You have had an opportunity
To read and see
That you can live
In victory.

You have been told
That you can soar
The height you can reach
Only the Savior knows.

So bury your old self
Become the new kid on the streets
Who is capable of handling
Anything he meets.

Who knows he is wonderfully made.
Is one of a kind.
Who is strong,
And have a well-made up mind.

You were born with a purpose
In God's image and likeness.
You are not dumb
Because of your hair or blackness.

You are more than a conqueror.
Who is unique and divine.
You can now succeed
Because you have renewed your mind.

(Continued)

You looked in the mirror
And whom did you see?
A person who is focused–
A man of destiny.

Who is willing to press on
And leave Egypt behind,
Cross over Jordan
And a new home found.

You can aboard your ship
That is about to sail.
Hang on to hope.
You will not fail.

God has given you wisdom.
You don't have to stand at the crossroad.
Lay down your burdens.
Let God carry your load.

He is bigger than your storm.
Let him take control.
Don't listen to the enemy.
Don't give him your soul.

Instead, listen to the voice of reason.
Can't you understand?
Be anxious for nothing.
You are in God's hand.

Throughout this book
You have been told
That you are somebody,
More precious than gold.

So take heed my child.
Why do you hesitate?
Get your back off the wall.
You don't have time to wait.

You are who God says you are.
You can obtain victory!
Soar high, my child–
Soar above adversities!

Pay no attention to the world.
Just let it be.
Your lost is not a defeat.
Soar! Soar above adversities!

Give it all to Jesus.
Let him set you free!
He has given you strength.
To soar above adversities.

Ordering Information

To order copies of this book, *Soar Above Adversities Inspirational Poems that Uplift the Spirit* or copies of *Letters to God and Other Poems that Touch the Heart*, *My Cup Runneth Over*, or to request a personalized poem contact the author at:

Nadene Cooper King
674 Della Glass Road
Smithville, Georgia 31787
229-846-4801
Fax: 229-846-4582
email: nadenek@netzero.net